JESUS DIDN'T GIVE UP ON ME

JESUS GAVE ME BACK MY LIFE

JOZLYN DANIELS

Jesus Didn't Give Up on Me

Published by: Tribune Publishers
www.tribunepublishers.com

Dedication

I could of never wrote this book without my greatest teacher Jesus Christ, He brought me to my knees to bring me back to life. Without him I would have never been able to look at my life and extract the lessons and turn them to my greatest advantage and strength. I could have never learned to love myself or others correctly. I would not be who I am today without letting him into my heart .

Acknowledgment

First, I need to thank Jesus Christ, as he has been my biggest supporter, teacher, and healer. Because of you I have my life back as I now know what true unconditional love is. I forever owe my life to you.

Thank you to Tribune Publishers team with helping me every step of the way of publishing my book.

I would like to thank David's parents for supporting me the last two years and becoming my family. I love you.

Philip, I can't thank you enough for coming into my life and helping me see what I needed to heal, Jesus used an angel in disguise.

Contents

Preface

My story isn't a poor me story, it's a real story. My story is about traumas I went through as a small child to drinking, drugs, bad decisions and actions I put myself into as a young adult that followed me into my late 40's. Until Jesus stepped in and saved my life. I wrote this book as Jesus asked me to, to show you that everything you go through in life happens for a reason. We just have to open our eyes and hearts to see and learn the lesson. I want everyone to believe miracles do happen every day. Don't ever give up hope on yourself or others. Your traumas and mistakes in your past do not define you. It's never too late to change. Believe in yourself as Jesus Christ believes in you. We are one.

Chapter One

LOSING MY INNOCENCE

Today I'm going to tell you the story of my life, my traumas, and what I've learned and healed from, From my childhood to my spiritual awakening.

I will just be giving you a quick version of some things but more in-depth of the important events.

I grew up in Michigan with both of my parents until I was 11 years old. We moved around a lot so we never really had a house to call home. I was sexually abused by my dad from the ages of 3 to 10 years old.

My mom and I never got along or had a bond even as a small child. She always acted jealous of the relationship I had with my dad. I never understood why, well I found out later on in life that my mom knew about the abuse and would threaten to call the cops and report the abuse if my dad left her. So my abuse could have been stopped but my mom kept it going just so she could have a man in her life.

With my dad sexually abusing me he used to take me everywhere with him. I thought it was because he loved me and wanted to spend time with me but as an adult I now see it was him trying to make sure I was happy and kept my mouth shut.

Out of both my parents, my dad was the one who made sure I was taken care of and fed though. So I had a love-hate relationship with him.

My sister was also being molested by my dad. We have different dads but I never looked at it like that. She is the one who told someone at school about the molestation. So my dad was sentenced to 5 years in prison. People often wonder why kids don't say anything about what is going on. Well, I can tell you why. Because you're terrified. Like my dad said to me, the threats I received were, you will break up the family or I will go to jail. That doesn't sound that scary for an adult to hear but to a small child, it's awful. Even though he is your molester he's still your father and now he's building a love-hate relationship with you.

When he went to court I had to get on the stand and identify him face to face. This needs to be changed. Kids are already traumatized and this adds another trauma on top of it. I'll never forget the look on his face. He looked sad and also his face was saying I can't believe you're doing this to me.

Children should be able to do this through a TV screen or pictures and testify and tell their story to the judge without the molester being in the room.

While my dad was in prison he was diagnosed with brain cancer. He was given 6 months to 1 year to live. But he did have brain surgery which prolonged his life another 5 years. He wrote to me when he was in prison but he never did admit to what he did or even say he was sorry, but he was trying to keep the relationship between us open. When I found out about his brain cancer I became depressed because I felt bad he was in prison because of me and now he was dying. I know it wasn't my fault it was his but as a 14-year-old that's how I felt.

When the depression hit I was living in foster care. My sister and I were both removed from my mom's care for neglect after my dad was gone. My foster parents were great people and a great family to have. They admitted me to a mental hospital when I got depressed which I got kicked out of because I turned all the kids against the staff. All they do is put you on medication and send you to some group counseling, it doesn't do anything for you. I was mad and told the counselors what they should be doing to help us. I didn't think you could get kicked out but yes you can.

When I was in foster care I was in counseling and Sharon did great with me, she helped me realize that what happened with my dad wasn't my fault and that most molesters were either molested themselves or had witnessed it happening in their family. This is the story with my dad, he had walked in on my grandpa molesting my aunt. Nobody knows for sure if he was molested or not. I also know of other incidents in our family so I'm assuming it runs deeper than what I know of. So this becomes a vicious cycle that doesn't stop until you put a stop to it once and for all.

But what my dad did to me as a child affected me in so many ways that I never truly realized until the last 2 years of my life. I'm now 48. I thought I was doing great in life pushing forward and not looking back. I WAS WRONG. When we are molested as children it's usually done by a family member or family friend so that automatically takes away our security. We are supposed to be protected as children, but it also makes us feel unseen, unheard, unloved, and insecure with ourselves and others. I felt like I was being punished which in return turned me into a people pleaser. We do this because we feel if we make everyone around us happy we won't be abandoned or hurt and they will keep loving us.

A lot of people become sexually promiscuous even though we are kind of disgusted by men after this. But you crave their attention only because you want a man to love and protect you. After all, we didn't receive this as a child. But in our subconscious because of the trauma, you think all men are liars, cheaters, playing games with you, out to hurt you, don't truly love you, and keep secrets which in most cases they are. Because broken people attract broken people. And when a good man does come along we self-sabotage because you're already expecting them to hurt you or leave you anyway.

Even though the molestation wasn't our fault we pay for it the rest of our lives. With the research I have done on the side effects of molestation, I was shocked to see I suffered from a lot of these. Here's a list of what I have found.

Unexplained changes in sleep and appetite- Fear of a person - watch the child's body language.-Bed wedding - Curious about sex or genital area more than normal -Fear -Self-conscious - Sadness Feeling low or irritable - worry a lot - low self-esteem - alcohol and or drug use - anger — withdrawal — guilt - self-blame anxious- thoughts of suicide- confusion -anxiety -self-harm feel humiliated - panic attacks — obsessions-don't like being touched - eating disorders -affect how they parent - overly protective -don't want to be a parent - will affect family and relationships with members even as kids - hypertension — fatigue- lose faith in Jesus — shame- education -feels future stolen from them -poor physical health careers- chance of them becoming victims again later in life- sexually promiscuous — gambling -spending too much money physically - how to hold a relationship- intimate and platonic -hard to communicate with everyone about the abuse-trust issues -hard time with intimacy not just sexually- embarrassed- angry with life and family members that knew- OCD can't control environment so control objects around them- memory loss- natural defense mechanism-self-sabotage-sabotage spouse because they can't fill void we feel-phobias-panic attacks - avoidant coping skills- keep distance to avoid getting hurt-hard to get close to others because we're denied the developmental skills and experiences so as adults survivors we often seek to avoid the attention and closeness of others in social contact - Completely disassociate the need to express pain - lack tools necessary to label properly- control others-waiting for something bad to happen- identities are formed by absorbing -thinking about how the attitudes behaviors and expectation of others around us reform our world-aggressive defensive — overly shy-feel alone- fear getting hurt or rejected-too clingy -overly dependent- most likely to be pulled into different or abusive relationships later in life -overly critical expecting too much of themselves or not expecting anything at all - people pleasers -pick up care taker roles -children can even go back to thumb sucking -running away - night sweats-nightmares and I'm sure there is more.

I do have to say it doesn't just have to be sexual abuse for these side effects I have also seen this in mentally, emotionally, and physically abused children.

RECOVERY BEGINS WITH THE TRUTH OF WHAT HAPPENED AND HOW IT HAS AFFECTED YOU

Chapter Two

FOSTER CARE

As I said earlier my mom and I never got along even as a small child. She was never a mentally or emotionally supportive person. She always seemed depressed and very negative about everything. Anytime my sister or I were excited about something going on she would always talk it down or bring up negative things about it that could happen. She was always ruining any joy we did have. I couldn't be around her long because I would have a pounding headache and exhausted. She would be what we call an energy vampire. I really can't say anything about my mom's past to know why she was like this because I never asked or cared.

But I can say she always worked and made sure we had a roof over our head though and that was important even though she was never there. When she wasn't working she was out with her best friend or having an affair with her best friend's husband. But as a child, my only good memory of my mom was she always made sure we had an excellent Christmas. And to this day I love Christmas because of those memories. By noon she was back to being crabby but the memories of her sticking candy under our pillow and she would come in and say looks like Santa Claus came. She had already been up and had the Christmas tree lights on and her coffee made. She would hand out Christmas gifts and we had to wait until they were all handed out. Then take turns opening presents so she could watch both of us. Those are memories I will never forget. As I sit here writing this I wonder if she did this to make up for the rest of the year because she always went overboard at Christmas.

Her parents from what I was told were the same way, not showing emotions. I got along great with my grandma but now that I think back she never hugged us either. But my grandma always made sure to go to my basketball and soccer games then she would take me to the Big Dipper for Superman ice cream afterward. I loved it. She was always sweet to us and I didn't know she wasn't good with emotions either but either way, she is the best memories I have as a small child. She passed away during the time of writing this book.

There was a time I was in foster care I could have gone home to my mom's but at the time my sister's ex-boyfriend was living there and they told her he would have to move out because of his violent history and she said no because I had a place to live he didn't. So I was now being abandoned by my mom. My mom has since passed away. I did go to her memorial but only to support my sister and nieces who were close to her.

When I was in foster care, my foster mom was a great woman, strong, independent but sometimes she would get quiet and kind of cold. When she would do this I would feel like she was mad and I would be walking on eggshells. I didn't know how to talk about it but I was young. But her pulling her energy back was very uncomfortable. My foster dad was a great man. He was a very hard worker and worked nights so I didn't see him as much as I would have liked. But they were the closest thing I had to a real family.

When I went to foster care I did have to switch Foster homes at one point because I got mad at my foster mom and told my caseworker I wanted to move but what I didn't realize is it would happen. So I broke my own heart. I didn't know at the time I was already self-sabotaging.

I went to another foster home that was okay but it was nothing like the one I had just left. I did make a couple of great friends there Tanya and Amber. I still keep in contact with Tanya but Amber we have both lost contact with over the years.

Tanya and I did get in trouble together one time. It was New Year's Eve her mother went out on a date so we took her mom's car down to the store, on the way back we hit a tree because of ice. They had to get the jaws of life to get me out and Tanya has had to have neck and back surgery because of this accident. We didn't get in trouble with the police but we sure got in trouble with her mom and my foster mom.

Tanya and Amber also came from troubled homes so we helped each other. We would get together and just laugh for hours. They made the new foster home bearable.

Another time my boyfriend and I ran away, we walked from Alpena to Standish (105 miles) stole a car from a bar and drove it to Cadillac. The car we stole was a stick shift which neither of us even had a clue on how to drive plus we were only 15 at the time. At one point we stalled it at a stoplight and a cop pulled up helped us push it out of the way then he got in his car and drove off.

When we decided to go back home we had court the next day and I was released to my mom's care because they said I would keep running away. I was hoping they would send me back to my first foster home but they didn't.

About 2 weeks later I took a whole bottle of Dilantin. I figured I had time so I ran over to my sister's house directly behind ours so I could see my sister and niece's really quick. But the next thing I know I woke up in the hospital getting my stomach pumped. I was 16 at the time and by this time I was already feeling lost and alone. Yes, my foster parents tried helping me with the counseling and I'm sure it did. But it wasn't enough because as a child you learn what everyone wants to hear so you tell them what they want to hear to get yourself out of counseling. It's sad to say. But it's the truth we learn how to manipulate the system. Just like we were manipulated.

Chapter Three

BAD CHOICES

A few months later I started dating Brian. He was a nice guy but not my type. But I was bored yes I know that's wrong but at the time I didn't think that way. But I figured I wouldn't have to be around my mom a lot. What I didn't plan on was getting pregnant. I was excited in a way because I was going to be a mom but in another way, I was scared because I didn't know how to be one since I never truly had a mom. Brian and I got married I felt like it was the right thing to do but I knew it wasn't what I wanted.

We had a short marriage, I was miserable and I didn't like feeling trapped. I'm sure not everyone feels that way but I did immediately. By the time our marriage was over we had two boys together.

During this time, my dad also died. I was 18 at this time and my drinking started the night after he passed away. Between everything in my life up until this point, then my dad dying it pushed me over the edge. I know it doesn't make it right but at this point, I felt done and overwhelmed. Brian and I were also going through a custody battle at the time and he did end up getting custody because he was older, working, and had his place. He did let me take the boys when I wanted plus we always lived close to each other.

I started dating Wayne whom I liked but Wayne was also a drinker. As you can guess it was a perfect match in my eyes. He was hot, sports car, liked to party, and had a good personality. Wayne and I partied all summer long but my drinking was taken over. I was drinking a fifth of vodka a day and then having to go into his beer. I couldn't stand beer but when you already drank a fifth of vodka the beer tasted like water at that point.

During this time, I quit seeing my boys so much because I was always drunk and I knew they were better off without me in their life. I didn't feel worthy of them.

Wayne and I did get married a couple of years later. This time I wanted to get married, we were married for 17 years. But I wasn't happy after a few years once again. There was infidelity in our marriage, drinking all the time, and a void I could not fill. All my life I felt like something was missing. And the older I got the more I felt it.

Wayne and I ended up splitting up because I cheated on him and I asked my mom and sister to watch our daughter for the weekend so I could move. Well, my mom wanted to claim her on her food stamps and taxes and I said no It was only for a weekend. So she called CPS on me thinking they would give her custody but of course, they told her no. But now I had a CPS case on me. I did slow down on my drinking before all of this. But CPS was using this against us.

We both had to do drug and alcohol evaluations, well I did mine first and I told the truth about my heavy drinking years previously and I was labeled a chronic alcoholic. This was crazy because at this point I was drinking one maybe two days a week and I always had an overnight babysitter because I didn't trust myself when I was drinking. I was always afraid something would happen. Wayne went and took his test he lied because of my results, he was labeled clear no problems at all and he was the one who was still drinking every day. Because of my results, I had to do breathalyzers twice a day, to get our visits with our daughter. We went through this for 3 years and during this time we had two more daughters.

My first daughter was living with my aunt instead of foster care, our second daughter went into foster care but her foster family were great people. We kept in contact all the time, even to this day. She even informed me that the CPS caseworker told her if you help me come up with a case against her parents you could keep their daughter. I was furious. But appreciated her honesty. With our third daughter, they were going to put her in foster care also, but a couple we met took her.

I was angry with myself, felt guilty, and seeing how we sabotaged everything. All together our kids were gone 3 years and there came a point where Wayne and I sat down and decided to let our girls get adopted. They were calling so many different people Mom and Dad and it wasn't fair to them. They needed a stable home without being shipped around with visits to different places and different homes. They needed a solid set of parents who weren't drunks. In the back of my head, I always thought this way no one could ever abuse them. I never told anyone that until a few years later.

We had to quit being selfish and let our kids have a good life. I'm trying to keep my kids out of the story as much as possible for their privacy but this was a major heartbreak. I will tell you I am in contact with most of my kids and grandkids. They didn't have to let me stay in their life but the parents and my kids allowed it and I'm very thankful for that.

Well, there came a point I had to be honest with myself and I knew it wasn't fair to stay in this marriage. I wasn't being fair to myself but it also wasn't fair to Wayne. He deserved to be with someone who could be in love with him. I kept feeling and thinking there had to be more to life. I felt empty all the time I tried different jobs, relationships, and experiences and nothing was filling that void that I was feeling. I used to just think I was bored in life but now I see I needed to heal on the inside. I wish I knew then what I know now. But I still had more lessons to learn, and more pain to endure, it finally got to a point where I told Wayne I wanted a divorce.

We were drinking that night and Wayne was driving our new car, He wasn't used to no play in the steering wheel like his work truck. We were going around a sharp corner he ended up going off the road flipping and hitting a tree. I don't remember much except being in the ambulance and the driver told the police officer to let Wayne come say goodbye because they weren't sure if I was going to make it. I told Wayne I don't know why they're saying that I'm fine. I didn't know the main artery in my arm was torn in half. I woke up in the morning with over 60 stitches. Wayne was in jail waiting for the hospital to call and say whether I lived or not. He did get sentenced to 6 months in jail with work release. We also did get divorced while he was in jail and we were able to stay friends through all of this until we both started dating other people.

So by this time, I had already broken 2 husbands' hearts and now I lost all my kids because I wasn't healing my childhood traumas or taking responsibility for any of my actions. But I can say that both ex-husbands went on into long-term relationships and as far as I know they are happy.

Chapter Four

DANCING WITH THE DEVIL

After Wayne, I started dating Floyd. Floyd's brother and I have been friends for years but I only knew Floyd in a few encounters when he was up visiting his brother. Floyd and I connected on Facebook and he was coming up in a couple weeks so we had plans to hang out. The next thing I knew he was moving up and we were going to be together. I thought holy cow this is fast but I liked him and thought this would be fun. His brother had told me he was crazy and even told me stories but not the kind of stories I experienced.

Shortly after he moved up the controlling, mental, and emotional abuse started. Within the next 3 months, the physical abuse also started. I was warned and should have paid attention. I don't smoke weed because I can't handle it. He told me I needed to build my tolerance up so I tried. So I did this for a year it never worked but one night we got high off my one hit and it was storming, it was thundering, and lightning out. I was looking at him and just as it was lightning I saw the devil's face clear as day. Scared me so bad, Jesus was trying to warn me. I talked myself into believing it was because I was high. But I was wrong.

Floyd wasn't always mean sometimes he loved me so hard and strong but in reality, this is how manipulators and narcissists work. In my head, I thought he must not have been loved in the right way or once he sees I won't leave him like his exes did then he will change. With abusive men, they mess with you kicking your ass, and loving you so hard after. It's a sick game they play with you. There are even times he would say things like look what you made me do or Why would you say that to make me so angry?

Before I knew it or realized what he was doing to me I was walking on eggshells. I used to get annoyed with women who stayed in relationships like this and now here I was in the middle of one. You don't realize that's what happens until it's too late. The reality is they do this on purpose to manipulate you to agree with them and for you not to ask questions or question them. When you ask questions they get mad because you are questioning their authority as they see it. Or you're trying to take your power back. Every time I would try to leave him he would cry and make me feel bad so I would feel like I was abandoning him and causing pain to someone then I would stop myself because I knew how it felt and I didn't want to do that to him.

It's strange to say but you get addicted to the highs and lows they create with you. Before you know it you crave the highs. There are too many violent stories to tell about this man but I will tell you a few. I will also tell you he figured it out at a young age that if he lost his temper and said he didn't feel good in the head he could get away with it. So anytime he would get violent they would send him to a mental hospital which he referred to as a vacation and laugh about it. He would say he is bipolar but yet he could control himself around anybody who he chose to. It's sad the mental health system is a failure not only to victims but also to people who truly have mental disorders.

With Floyd I have had loaded shotguns to my head, knives to my throat, choked out, kicked in the face and I can go on. The night this all changed was a night he did a karate kick to my face. He was a two-time black belt. So he knew exactly what he was doing. I should have left when he was at the mental hospital but his young son was there. I went in his room after Floyd went to jail and he had tears in his eyes. He asked me I'm not going to turn out like my dad am I? I said no absolutely not he asked how do you know? I explained how he was loving and caring and how he cared about other people. And how he was so much better than his dad. I named off all his good qualities. It was cute because, after our conversation every time he came over for the weekend, he would climb up next to me and ask why do you love me more than you do my dad? And I would repeat it all over again and I was happy to do it. I wanted to make sure he knew he was nothing like that man.

But the night Floyd kicked me in the face he had called the cops on himself before I even walked in the door. I didn't believe him of course so when I ran to the phone he wasn't running after me which surprised me. When I picked up the phone the 911 operator was on the other line and she said ma'am stay on the phone I asked what did he say to you? She replied I'm homicidal suicidal get here before I kill her. Before I knew it my house was surrounded by cop cars. When I went back outside here was Floyd sitting in his chair smoking a joint and already had his mental hospital bag packed. Sure enough, he only got a week's vacation out of it.

This incident happened because I went to the park with a co-worker and her two small children. He was angry because I took time away from him and wanted to have girl time. He called 72 times in a 4-hour period but because I took my power back away from him and did what I wanted this is what I received.

A week later he was back from his vacation and I was cooking dinner before his son went back to his mom's. Floyd got mad about something I said, he picked up a butcher knife and started running at me but this time I didn't move out of the way or run. The fear was gone that I used to have. As he got close to me he stopped and yelled what are you stupid? I laughed and said no I'm not scared of you anymore. I think that is what he thrived on. If you want to kill me go for it. I'll be in heaven while you're in prison getting raped by men. He was furious but this is a day I figured I would give him a taste of his own medicine.

I turned into him, I never got violent but I became the heartless shell who didn't care what came out of my mouth. I became the anger, hatred, and the pain. Floyd was the kind of person who could say cruel things but if you said them back he would get so angry or even cry. Even if it's exactly what he just got done saying to you. I made sure to be cruel every day. My goal was to hurt him like he had hurt me and I did just that. But in reality, I hurt myself because I became him. I didn't know at the time I was self-sabotaging myself by staying in this relationship that was changing me and not for the better. But at the same point, they beat you down enough that you don't see your self worth. You become afraid to leave because you know that they will come after you. But there comes a time you have to take that chance. You can only dance with the devil for so long.

Chapter Five

BAD PLAN

I came up with a plan to move to Florida. We were going to move down there and my plan was going to skip out and move back so he wouldn't be able to find me. I knew if we were in the same town this would never end. Well, when we went down his son came down a couple of days later, he was only supposed to be down for a couple of weeks so I was stuck until he went home.

Well, when it came time for him to leave, I called his mom for the plane ticket and she informed me she didn't want him to come back he was going to stay with us. I was furious. I wanted to go home. I know he wasn't my child, but in my heart he was and I had to protect him. Anytime I would leave he would call me crying because Floyd was going after him so I would go back to stop it. I had talked to his mom many times about it but she was newly married and Floyd's son and the new husband didn't get along.

So now I had to come up with a new plan. In the meantime, I started up a cleaning and painting business. Thanksgiving was getting close so I held a turkey drive for people in need. This is how I met Jason.

Jason was a great guy who I ended up doing some work for. We would have great conversations and we laughed so much. I haven't laughed in a long time. So, he was a breath of fresh air.

When I was over there we would laugh and talk for hours and after a while, we started doing coke together. We started to really like each other. He wanted me to leave Floyd but I couldn't because of his son. I kept saying I would but then the fear would kick in. I did end up marrying Floyd because I needed the medical insurance which he knew but I told him I wanted a divorce after my procedure.

But I came up with moving back to Michigan for a doctor's reason and I figured I'd leave him there and come back down. But this way I could get his son back to his mom's somehow. So, I knew he was taking care of, it was a win-win.

I had the house sold in Florida in 3 days and bought a house in Saginaw. I stayed up there and helped remodel the house so that way all the money was spent on his house but then he couldn't come look for me. I also got to spend time with my kids.

I rented a storage unit and would act like I was donating things to Goodwill. In reality, I was putting it in boxes in the storage unit and when a box was full, I would send it down to Jason's house. I had it planned out I was going to act like I was going to work. When in reality I was going to hop on a plane. Well, his great-grandma happened to pass away the same week I was leaving. I didn't want anybody to die but it worked out to be the perfect getaway. When he left to go to the funeral I drove to the airport and left. I didn't change my address because I didn't want him to find me but I was free. I was finally going to be happy. I WAS WRONG.

Chapter Six

LOST MY HOPE

It was on a Friday in January when Jason picked me up at the airport. We were both very excited to see each other. We partied all weekend long and did some coke. We talked for hours; it was like I had never left. That Saturday Jason asked me to marry him for about the fifth time and of course, I said yes. He used to tell me I was going to marry him even before we started dating. Sunday night we relaxed, about 6:00 we put a roast in the oven. We laid down, I set the alarm to wake up at 9:00 so we could eat. I got up to turn the oven off and laid back down. I woke up at 2:00 a.m. and Jason was facing the other way. I then woke up again at 6:00 am but this time when I woke up I knew something was wrong before I even rolled over. I whipped around and when I looked at Jason, I knew he was dead.

I jumped to my knees shaking him. I think it was an automatic reaction. His face was blue on the side so he had been dead for a while. I called 911 and ran outside so they didn't miss the house. I was so happy to see them come around the corner. They rushed in and when they looked at him, they said I'm sorry there's nothing we can do. I asked well can't you electric shock him or something? They said no he's been dead too long.

Then his mom popped into my head and I thought oh my God I have to call her. I couldn't find my phone but I found Jason's phone again and called his sister and his mom. Those are phone calls I'll never forget. The screams haunted me for weeks. As I'm writing this it brings tears to my eyes. I had only met his mom a couple of times but I loved her from day one. After hours of sitting at the house answering questions and waiting for them to come get Jason's body, it was finally over.

I remember going back into the house and wondering what to do now? We had so many plans and now they were gone. Jason was my best friend. One of his hugs would have taken care of anything at that moment. I went and cleaned up then went out to his mom's house. When I pulled up his brother David was outside. It was the first time I had met him in person. Jason never spoke highly of David but I didn't see anything wrong. From what I was told he had a history of being in and out of rehab and jail.

His parents weren't going to let David go to Jason's funeral they said he would have caused problems. The way they were talking he sounded like a small child. I told them he could sit with me which he did and had no issues.

David and I ended up hanging out for a few months. Then we had another memorial at Jason's mom's for his family and friends here. During this time, I found out Jason cheated on me while I was in Michigan so I was hoping his friend would show up that he cheated with but she didn't. Now I'm glad that she didn't. I was angry and hurt but I understood it because I was up there for a while.

But that night I got drunk and David and I kissed. He used to come to his brother's house and we would Ghost Hunt because there were weird things happening. It started out I was sleeping on the couch and I woke up to someone kissing me. Well, I jumped up because there was no one in the house. When I looked over, I saw Jason's legs walking away from me. I busted out in tears because I wanted him to stay.

This isn't the first time I have seen a spirit. I was 7 years old the first time I was with my dad, Uncle, cousin, and sister on Thanksgiving Day. This man was standing there next to the road. He was glowing, he was just looking at us as we drove by. I remember asking my dad if he was going to stop and see if he needed help because he always helped people. He asked me who I was talking about. I said the man you just passed. He looked in his rear-view mirror and said there was no one there. I turned around and said he's right there. But no one could see him except for me. I got angry because I thought they were messing with me. Throughout my life, this wasn't uncommon to see spirits but I didn't know that's what I was seeing as a child.

Well, it took about 3-4 months to get Jason's autopsy results back and he had overdosed. Jason had been in a couple of motorcycle accidents and was on OxyContin plus we had coke that weekend. I knew he had a problem with the oxy. But I also knew he was working on that when I was gone.

After this incident, David really wanted to try to contact Jason through his ghost-hunting devices. Well, David was really big into rituals I had no experience with anything like this. But one night he asked me to help him, and I said sure. He wanted me to come carve a design into the wood and he asked me for my necklace. I said no because it was from Jason. He said I will give it right back so I gave it to him. He stuck it under a large candle. So, I grabbed the pencil and when I started carving, I stopped and looked under the candle and the necklace was still there. But when I went back to carving something was between my hand and the pencil. I looked and it was my necklace dangling. My mouth dropped. We looked at each other and decided we were done for the night.

A few days later he was back over, we were talking about what happened the other day and he said something about demons. I laughed and I said demons are a joke. He got very upset. He started arguing with me I thought this was crazy. But I wasn't backing down. I said yes Jesus has my back. He was at my house until 6:00 that morning going to do a ritual to call demons forward. So I was being sarcastic and was offering advice. Which made him even more upset. After a while, he gave up.

We didn't talk for a few days after this. I should have never talked to him again. But again, I felt bad for him and thought I could help him. A few nights later I said I wanted to go to Palm Bay to get some coke. He said no I know where we can get some speed, well when we got there it was meth. I made him smoke it first because I wanted to see how he acted on it. When I smoked it, I didn't realize how this was going to affect me for the next couple of years. I wanted to numb the pain I was in and this worked. David's parents could tell when he was on drugs so they had him Baker acted about a month later. When he went into rehab they drug-tested him. He showed positive for all 12 drugs at extremely high levels. So that tells you what they put in that. When he was in rehab, I stayed on it so as you can guess when he got out he was right back on it. We started dating during this time.

Within a few weeks, strange things were happening around the house. David and I set up cameras to see if we could catch anything. I have got some really crazy pictures of paranormal activities. The landlord had them looked at because she thought they were fake; she was shocked to find they were not edited.

During this time, I was still very depressed about Jason. But one night I took one of Jason's guns outside in the driveway and I put the gun up to my head and I pulled the trigger. When I shot the gun it went upward and missed going through my skull. I had the gun directly lined up so there was no reason it missed. But I ran into the house and woke David up and told him he had to leave because if you have a felony, you can't be around guns and David had a felony so he was flipping out but wouldn't leave. Luckily the cops didn't show up. The area I lived in was packed with houses and cops were always there. Jesus saved me that night.

A couple of days later I was arrested for meth possession. David and I were down on a road by the river. I told him to hurry up before the cops showed up. No longer did I get those words out of my mouth and sure enough the cops showed up.

Neither of us knew we were on private property. But somehow I knew something bad was going to happen. It was my first and last drug charge on my record. I had 2 DUI's from when I was drinking in my 20's and a B & E that I didn't even go in the house but I was in the car on the property so I still got charged. With my meth charge my lawyer said I was going to get a year in jail because of a point system here in Florida so I fired him and hired a lawyer. I ended up with 1 year of probation. Right before I was supposed to get off probation I got caught driving without a license and in Florida, if you're on probation it's automatically 30 days in jail.

While I was in jail I kept hearing as above so below. I didn't have a clue what that meant but at this time I still didn't understand That after Jason died, I was going through a spiritual awakening. But it means bringing heaven onto earth, which is taking the hell out of your head and healing you.

Then one night I had a dream that Jason and I were in a room with black and white checkered flooring. The floor pieces were moving opposite of each other and I could see the sky below them. Jason had his hand held out with his fist closed. I told him to stay there and I would come to him. We were both falling all over the place. When I finally got to him, he dropped my cross necklace in my hand. At that time, I couldn't figure out what this dream meant. But now I do, the dream meant that I better find Jesus I was on shaky ground. I should have listened.

A few weeks later David and I were sitting in the bedroom and I was mad and I was worried about him because he started doing subs. And he would do things he shouldn't be. I was telling him I am not going to be the one to call his mom and tell her another son died. All of a sudden, he looked at his plate of ravioli and said what the hell but he sounded like Jason. Then he looked at me and said what are you doing here? He picked up his hand and flipped it over observing It. Then he said I've been here before. A second later he jumped and had a panicked look on his face and back in David's voice he said what the hell just happened? I replied I don't know. He said my ravioli turned into spaghetti; my hand was big like Jason's. I remember looking at you but it shocked me you were here. And I thought why am I back here? He said but it wasn't me I was Jason. The crazy part is David never knew I had the same conversation with Jason while Jason was eating spaghetti. Somehow Jason jumped into David's body for a moment.

Chapter Seven

WHAT IF

David and I ended up moving into the cottage next to his parent's house that they had remodeled. It was weird because at the house we had just left, David had done a lot of maturing. But as soon as we moved to the cottage David turned back into this immature man I had met. I was hoping I could turn him back around.

As soon as we moved there, I had a weird feeling that David was cheating on me. He swore he wasn't. I was finding porn on his phone, weird phone numbers, and dating sites. He always denied that they were his. He actually got to the point where he said it was his dad hacking his account to cheat on his mom. When I didn't believe that, he turned it into it was me doing it to make it look like he was cheating. So I had something to be mad about. He would shed tears or even throw fits to prove it wasn't him. He would argue his point so much that, at times he had me thinking I was crazy. After a while, it became a game between us; I had to prove I was right he was cheating, and he played to see what he could get away with. It was a game neither of us could give up by this point. Things were getting pretty toxic.

A year later, David and I went to Michigan to help work on my daughter's new house.

Well, from the moment we got off the plane, he was acting weird. Then, one night we got into an argument. He said my granddaughter might have to be sacrificed. I was furious, and my head went to a time when Jason told me that David dabbled on the dark side. I had asked David about this previously, and he denied it. But he got in my face. I pushed him back because I couldn't stand that from being with Floyd. But he picked me up, body slamming me to the floor.

When I got up, he was in the bathroom going through his suitcase and looking for his meds, which he had already taken. He was on ADHD meds which we always had to keep away from him or he would take them all. I grabbed the suitcase and when I did he got hit in the nose. The next thing I knew, he tackled me to the ground and was choking me. He had his hand wrapped around my throat, squeezing so tightly I was trying to get my fingers between his hand and my throat so I could breathe. I was thinking oh my God, I'm going to die in my daughter's house before she even moved in. I thought to myself tell him you love him. So I did, in a weird voice he said no she don't she's lying, I said no I'm not. In the strange voice, he said don't believe her, she's going to put you in jail. I replied no, I won't. He finally released me. I got up, went out to the car, and took off. It was late at night I didn't know where I was, so I finally found my way back to the house. I sat in the driveway with the doors locked until day light. I so badly wanted to put him in jail, but I didn't because I didn't want to hurt his mom like that. He had already put them through so much but with him being 1400 miles away I didn't want to make things worse for them. We ended up going to a hotel the rest of the week, he was fine there.

We got back to Florida I never said anything to his mom about it. The following weekend I found more porn on his computer. We had another fight, and David was getting in my face. His mom got in between us she said you put your hands on her and I'll put your ass in jail. He said oh, I already did that last weekend. He told them everything. After the fight calmed down, I found out the next day he had put a meth pipe in my toolbox. I was furious. He said I figured if you were going to call the cops on me you were going to jail too. But what he doesn't realize, or maybe he did, is that I would have gone to prison. I done decided after this that I was done. As soon as I was done with this job that Friday, I was going to take the money and leave. He knew I was done. So, the rest of the week, he was kissing ass.

One night, I came home, and the house was completely quiet and dark, so I figured he was gone. I went in the bedroom and grabbed clothes to shower and I heard someone crying. I went in the bathroom and David was on the floor in fetal position just sobbing uncontrollably. I asked him what was wrong? He said I saw it all, I saw everything. I asked what are you talking about? David replied it took forever to find you in this lifetime it's going to take longer next lifetime.

I was a little annoyed because the way he was crying I thought somebody had died or something, but instead he was being weird or so I thought. I sat there awhile to calm him down. I told him he must have fallen asleep and had a dream. But did he?

The next week when I was at work he had thrown away all of his belongings except for his clothes which he would never do that. But I didn't notice this because I never went out to his shed.

The next day he wanted to swap cameras. I said when I get home, we will go out and compare them. They were both expensive cameras. I said do not take it outside. The reason I said this is, David always lost everything. I cannot explain to you what he did with it because I don't even know, but he would lose things within minutes of getting his hands on things. I stopped at home at lunch, and sure enough, my camera was gone. I was so mad I walked in the bedroom and back to the kitchen and he was standing there. He had run in the house to put my camera back thinking I didn't notice yet. We started fighting. I yelled at him I said I can't stand you and I left.

That night around 6:00 I came home and I was still in the car. I heard David's motorcycle drive slowly behind me which was weird for him. I didn't look up but I did look on my passenger seat and notice that I forgot to drop some stuff off at Goodwill.

So, I went to Goodwill and through McDonald's and right back home. I didn't hear David's motorcycle or see him. When David was outside you could always see or hear where he was because of lights and music playing. But I didn't think much of it because his daughter was here for Christmas, so I figured he was with her somewhere. Well, we couldn't find him, so about 10:00 at night his dad went to the shed but it was so dark out he couldn't see anything. When he turned to go back into the house, he said he barely saw the motorcycle tail light but he caught a small glimpse of it. So, he went to make sure David didn't leave the keys in it like he had a bad habit of doing. Well, when he bent down to check the ignition, he felt David on the bike. He wasn't moving. His dad ran up to my house and told me he was unconscious. I grabbed a flashlight ran down there, I pulled the covid mask off his face, his lips were blue and his eyes were rolled back. I screamed for his dad because he went into the house to get David's mom. I didn't realize when I screamed, they were right next to me on the other side of the bush.

I remember I pulled him off his motorcycle and got him on the ground so we could start CPR. His mom asked if he was dead, I said yes. 911 was on the way. When they showed up, they said sorry it's too late he's been dead for a while. All I could think was why didn't I go down there and check?

I know why I didn't. I was mad at him, and like I said, you could always hear where he was, and it was silent when I got home that night. I thought he had left with his parents to open presents at his sister's house. But now I lived with

WHAT IF I HAD GONE TO HIS SHED?

So, his Mom lost her second son in 2 years, his dad lost his only child, his daughter lost her dad, and I lost my second boyfriend in 2 years. Even though we had our problems I loved him. I remember going to the house looking up at the sky and screaming I hate you I really hate you. I was so angry that Jesus did this for the second time. Then, the memory of the last words I said to David came rushing back.

It doesn't matter how angry we get at people words are something you can never take back they cut like a knife and leave scars. They last forever, and as I learned you never know if they are the last words you will say to that person.

Chapter Eight

MESSAGES FROM THE OTHER SIDE

The next day, I kept feeling the nudge to look in certain spots to find things he wanted me to find, to him appearing in front of me. I would even wake up to him sitting at the end of my bed.

David knew he was going to die without actually knowing. Or did he know? Since there were no obvious signs of why he died when we found him. Now I was thinking suicide of some sorts. I would have never thought this, but with a lot of this stuff gone, it had to be. But that just didn't seem like him, especially with his 8-year-old daughter here.

3-4 months later, we received his autopsy results back, and he had fentanyl in his system and a heart problem. We never found out where he got the fentanyl from and most likely never will.

But I honestly feel the night I came home to him in the bathroom crying, I think he saw his own death, and he wasn't being weird like I had thought. David had spiritual gifts; he had a vision of our past lives together. There were so many things he used to tell me that I wish I would have paid more attention to. So many things he said has happened since he passed away. When some people are different a lot of times it's because they are gifted and don't know how to handle it.

The next day, I was sitting on the couch, and I closed my eyes, and David walked in. He said Hey Kitty (that was my nick name) I said nope not today. I said I knew about all the lies. (I had found out after he died by doing a truth spell that I found online that yes David had been cheating not with just 1 person but multiple) He said I know that's why I'm back we have a book to finish. I said David, you're dead, he said no, we still have chapters to write. I said David we can't you're gone. (I was thinking he didn't know he was dead) He replied no I'm not. Then he draped a white sheet over us and kissed me. As I opened my eyes I was looking right at him and then he disappeared. I know you're thinking, oh, you fell asleep, but when I opened my eyes, I was looking directly into his. Anytime something happened in our relationship, he would always tell me we were starting a new chapter in our relationship. I couldn't figure out why he would be saying this when he was dead. I didn't realize he would be guiding me from the other side. I get signs and messages from him all the time.

As you can imagine this was a really tough time in my life. I just wanted to die. I used to think what did I do to deserve all this in my life? I was still smoking meth at the time to numb all the pain but it wasn't helping. And no what I was experiencing was not from the meth. Meth did not affect me the way it does some people. I was still working, I acted normal you couldn't even tell I was on it. It basically just gave me more energy.

One morning, I woke up to a man's voice saying, "You made me cry last night." I sat up because once again, no one was supposed to be there. But no one was in the house. So, I grabbed my phone on the bed to make sure I didn't roll over and accidentally call someone. But no, it wasn't that either. It was Jesus's voice he saw what I was doing and it was breaking his heart. You're probably wondering how I know it was Jesus, well I can tell you it's not the first time he has talked to me. He talks to us all the time. We just don't realize it. But this time it was very clear.

I always had my TV on with music playing. Certain songs would turn all the way up by themselves. Jelly Roll - Save me, Jelly Roll - Only, and Keisha- Praying. It was only those three songs at first, and then Kane Brown

-Homesick did it a couple of times. I thought maybe at first it was David trying to communicate with me. Later on during my spiritual Awakening I found out it was the Angels trying to get ahold of me to start praying and find Jesus because I was next.

Spiritual awakenings usually happen when a traumatic event happens in your life. I wish I would have known this right after Jason died. I would have gotten the signs a lot sooner. But the angels have been trying to get my attention for a while.

For the next 3 months, things got extremely crazy. I was getting drunk every day without drinking. It got to the point where I wouldn't even drive anymore because I was afraid, I was going to kill someone. But I kept working to stay busy.

I went to see a couple psychics during this time to try to figure out what was going on. I talked to Ann Fisher in New York she was amazing; she has helped the police on many cases and also told them a serial killers name and come to find out she was right.

She told me how David wanted me to help with his daughter and told me about David's ex-wife being crazy. Which yes, she was. She had been married 7 times, she set one of her husband's up, shot and killed him. David was her next husband after him, and she also shot him, but he lived through it. She was in the Navy, so she said self-defense on the 1st husband she killed and got away with it. With David she tried same thing an almost got away with it. She only got 12 months' probation but no contact with David. Well, David's dad saw a text message on his cell phone from her wanting David to sneak in a window to come see her instead of through the door. His dad turned her into her probation officer, so this time, she went to prison for 18 months. We all think she wanted him to sneak through the window so she could shoot him again and say he was coming after her. After this, David had PTSD and was paranoid about everything, which was understandable.

Explains a lot of problems we had. He always accused me of things that I didn't have a clue what he was talking about. After his death, I have learned that his ex-wife would do those things to him.

Chapter Nine

DARKEST DAYS

About a month later, I was talking to a friend of mine, Philip, through text. I met Philip about a month after I moved to Florida when I moved down to Florida with Floyd. Philip was always a great helpful friend who always helped me through many things even if it was just talking.

Philip was telling me his neighbor wanted her house painted, so I said I would stop there the next day. Well, that night he had text and said he would stop over at his neighbors and give me a few tips. I jokingly said tips with clothes on or clothes off. We had this relationship where we would joke around but I had never joked like that. And to this day I don't know why I did it that night? Well, a second later I got a text back that said clothes off, of course, and I texted back, lol. Put my phone down to go shower well when I got out of the shower there is a text that said this needs to be discreet, very discreet and I was shocked. I thought what the hell is he talking about? But I just texted back, LOL, and then a minute later, he was talking like we were going to have an affair. Which I thought was crazy because that's just not him. I really don't remember much about that conversation after that because I was shocked. I guess.

The next day I went over to his neighbors got the job and then he came over and helped a couple days. Philip and I clicked from the moment we met. He was funny and easy to get along with. Philip hired a lawyer one time when I was in jail to get me out. He was always helping me and was just an all-around good man. I was cleaning their house during all of this so we had become really good friends. His wife I never understood how they were together but I always thought well opposites attract.

When I was over at his neighbor's working, he knew something wasn't right with me mentally. I ended up telling him about the meth and that it was not a big deal. I could be off of it within a week. Well, the next day he showed up telling me that he did some research and from what he was telling me I was like oh shit. But I brushed it off.

I was telling him that day how I just didn't feel right in the head and that I was getting drunk every day without drinking. Well, next time I seen him he was telling me about some band he had watched and noticed these beads that the drummer was wearing on his wrist. When he went to his doctor appointment his Doctor was also wearing them. The beads turned out to be for healing and protection from evil spirits. So, Philip found a spiritual shop in our area, and we went there to get these bracelets. We also found out the shop owner was a Shaman and she was going to do a spiritual cleansing on me. Because of all the things we found out David was doing when he was alive. We thought maybe he had put something on me or was attached to me somehow.

I had to wait a couple weeks for the cleansing. In the meantime, my depression was getting worse. One night, the woman who was working for me was at my house. She left to go next door, and when she left, it felt like something came down and hit me in the chest. The only thing I could think was suicide.

I went into the bedroom. I was going to write out a text to all my kids and have them sent out at a certain time. I didn't want to call them because I knew I would back out. But I was going to go to the neighbors down the road and get some heroin. I was going to go across the street out into the woods, shoot it up, and make sure it was enough that it would kill me right away. I didn't do this drug I knew my body wasn't used to it so it would work. I was going to have a note here so when David's parents came over and noticed that I wasn't here they would find the note. I was going to tell them not to come out there, to send the cops out there to get my body. I didn't care I was ready to go.

I remember sitting on the bed and a song came on and I thought I wonder what it feels like when you die? Do the lights just go out? I sent Philip a text and said what does it feel like when the lights go out? He thought I was referring to a song so he sent me back a title and artist. I said no what's it feels like when the lights go out? He was over at my door about 15 minutes later.

We went for a ride and he said you know those movies where the person's eyes are black and they can turn their head all the way around? He said I remember you looked at me in the car I wanted to get out and run but I knew I couldn't. I later found out this was my dark night of the soul which is part of your spiritual awakening. The reason I was feeling drunk was because my soul was fragmented and I was going through an ego death.

The next day was my spiritual cleansing. I wanted to back out because I didn't feel like going. I didn't think it was going to do any good, but I kept feeling the nudge to go and I'm glad I did. When I left her shop, I could walk, talk and think straight, I felt fantastic. I hadn't felt that in months.

She did tell me that my ancestors had to step forward and help cleanse me. She said the best way to describe it was like a sticky tar that they pulled off of me.

That night, I kept walking around in circles, saying what the hell? I couldn't figure out why I was doing this, but when I talked to the Shaman a couple of weeks later, she explained it was because I was so used to carrying around trauma, anxiety, and depression, that with it being lifted off of you, now you don't know what to think or feel. I was happy it only lasted one night.

I had three other people get spiritual cleansings done and they all did the same thing. So, if you have never had one, I would definitely recommend it. But make sure they are real Shamans and know what they are doing.

I found out during my awakening Jesus sent Philip into my life during this time to save my life. If Jesus hadn't done this, I wouldn't be here today. I know that for a fact. Philip and I had been good friends, but not like this. Jesus guides people without us even knowing. The fact that Phillip noticed those bead bracelets watching a video. Then his Doctor happen to be wearing them, directed him to looking up spiritual shop right before he saw me and what was going on with me. If you ever notice something that you normally wouldn't or feel a nudge in a certain direction, always follow it through. Jesus doesn't nudge for no reason.

Chapter Ten

MY BIGGEST LESSON

During all of this, Philip and I were hanging out all the time. He was at my house a lot making sure I was ok. I truly appreciated it because I didn't have anyone else. My family is all in Michigan.

Philip and his wife were both unhappily married. So, neither of them cared he was gone all the time. That's all that I'm really going to say about that, as it is their marriage.

But at the same time, I loved and respected him for what he was doing, helping me through everything. I never had anyone help me through things in life I was always on my own. Philip was my normal, older, mature, well-off as in taking care of things, and wasn't abusive friend. He is actually very protective over women, kids, and animals, which was attractive to me because I am the same way. But he was that protector I always looked for. We used to laugh about everything, and he was my best friend.

Philip filed for divorce, and we decided to try to give our relationship a chance. We decided to get a place together. I was happy and scared at the same time. Because of everything I just went through.

Well, things were going good for a couple weeks but he kept going over to their house where his soon to be ex-wife lived. He said he had to go check his mail, and he wanted to see their dog. They had a dog together for 11 years, and I knew he missed and loved Bridget. I get it because I have fur babies also, and I would miss them terribly. But I was getting mad because I couldn't understand why he didn't grab the dog and bring her over for the day. He said he couldn't because she was a bulldog and they don't do well with separation and Bridget clamed Philips wife. There were days I was mad, but there were days I said go see the dog because I knew he missed her. I understood, but my insecurities were getting the best of me. I was jealous, and the fear of him going back kicked in.

This was a big problem I had. It made me feel very insecure, and all I kept thinking was if he wanted to be there so bad, why doesn't he just go back there? Then, I was accused of causing problems and trying to control him. I still say he's wrong. He was disrespecting me and shouldn't have left her until he was actually ready to. I don't think either of us thought everything through.

Philips divorce papers were supposed to be served before we even moved into the place we had together, but for some reason, they weren't. He ended up fighting with the place he hired to get a refund. He actually filed for divorce twice during our time together, but both times it was stopped. Well I received messages it was because he still had karma to serve with her. So it was wrong timing.

Philip and I would do some jobs together, but my work also slowed down at this time so I was at home a lot. I had a Lazer at our house so I was always keeping myself busy doing that. A lot of nights, I would stay up late working, and he would say something here and there about it, but then I would make remarks about going to his other house all the time to turn it back on him instead of owning up to my neglect that I was doing. Sometimes, it's so easy to dish it out, but when people call us out, we get defensive and try to turn the tables. I see these actions now. I wasn't able to at the time. This is what society calls the Darvo effect, which I picked up from being with Floyd who was a narcissist. I also talked to David's parents and found out David was diagnosed as a narcissist, but I didn't know this at the time.

One night we got back from metal detecting, and the phone rang, and he didn't answer it. I asked who's that? He replied you don't want to know. So I knew it was his wife. The phone rang again and it was her. I said you better answer it; it's probably about Bridget (their dog) he answered it and sure enough, Bridget had died. He left to go see the dog and to say goodbye.

I was worried when he left because we were in the middle of a hurricane, but I understood. Well, I did get upset when I found out he drove his dog and his wife back to Palm Bay to the vet so the dog could get cremated. I understood this part as we lived in Palm Bay. I was upset that he brought his wife, too. So now he had to drive her all the way back home in the storm. I didn't think it was right he was putting his life on the line for her. She could have said goodbye to their dog, and he could have just come home after he took Bridget to the cremation center. We ended up in an argument over this. Maybe I was wrong to feel this way; I'm still not sure. I admit I had control issues because of my past, But I was more concerned with his safety.

During this time, I was also trying to get off of meth. I tried slowing down and tried weaning myself off, but that didn't work. I even had Philip hold it and give it to me only when I truly needed it. This was awful. I thought quitting wouldn't be so hard, but I was getting brain zaps, my heart was pounding hard, my body was numb feeling, and my mood swings were crazy. Just not what I expected. He ended up giving it all back to me when we were fighting over the dog situation.

A few days later, his nephew passed away. When I came home from work, before I walked in, I knew he had taken off to New York without talking to me, leaving a note, or anything. So, I sent him a text, and sure enough, he did, which caused an even bigger fight. The reason was, well, we were fighting anyway. If I would have done that to him he would have been so angry.

During this time, I lied to him about somethings and I did it because I wanted him to stay. I knew we were going to split up. Stupid I know but I was trying to be important to him.

Philip left not only because of the lies, but he was also paying everything because my jobs stopped and I didn't have any money coming in. Philip had a house and a wife at home that he could depend on to pay half the bills, so he was smart and saved himself. He used to say it was to save us so we each had a roof over our heads, and I would laugh and say no, it's to save yourself. Rent was paid up for another 6 months, so the answer was clear. But I understood it. He just had a hard time admitting it.

Chapter Eleven

THE TRUTH HIT ME

Philip would still come over to visit. Then he said he was going to New York to visit his daughter, so while he was there, I was moving my stuff out, moving back to the cottage. When he left, I thought it was really strange. I was totally heartbroken, which blew my mind because that's not me, we weren't together long enough to be this heartbroken. I thought well maybe I loved him more than I knew I did.

That night, I was playing with my tarot cards, which for some reason I was really drawn to during all this. I had never had anything to do with tarot cards before but now I had a strong pull to them. But spiritual Awakening kept coming up. I didn't have a clue what it was, and I just went about my business packing up. I got an 8-ball of meth that night and a bong. I was going to smoke that whole thing because I didn't care if I lived or died. I never smoked like that. I didn't want to care about anyone or anything anymore. All it ever did was turn into heartbreak. I smoked the whole 8 ball that night. I remember trying to get off the bed, and I couldn't even walk or see straight. I remember telling Jesus to either kill me or take this from me because I can't do this anymore.

Later that day, I realized that I hadn't smoked all day, and I thought oh great, now that I realized it I'm going to. When I got home, I still had no cravings, I thought it was really strange. In my head all I kept hearing was you have work to do. Well, I have been completely drug-free now for

20 months no cravings or withdrawals, no nothing. Jesus took my drug addiction.

But there was a day I was having a rough time, and I got ahold of my dealer, and I drove there to buy some. But at the last minute I decided not to. I stopped to get gas, and as I was pumping my gas, sure enough my dealer pulled up. So, I bought some. I swear I was being tested. When I got home, I opened the bag and dumped it down the drain and broke the pipe. Never in my life did I think I would ever do this. But I had promised myself and Jesus I would never go back and I had to keep that promise. Also, I forgot to mention when I was married to Wayne, we were also snorting ridlin at the time on top of my drinking. Then, when I got with Floyd, he absolutely forbids the drinking, so I had really started snorting ridlin and hid it from him. So, it just recently hit me that 27 years out of my 48, I was using drugs or drinking.

Well, that night I decided to look up Spiritual Awakening again, when I got to the dark night of the soul is when I knew that's exactly what was happening to me. When I read up on it, it said if you surrender to it, it's a lot easier. I remember I sat back on the couch and I said Well heck if that's all I have to do I surrender. I'm not joking when I say I saw a line right in front of my eyes go through the house and all the noises stopped, the creaking stopped, I didn't see any shadow people in my house because I was seeing all this for a couple days.

I have gotten messages that I have actually been on this spiritual journey now for a couple years. My Spiritual Awakening started after Jason died and I have now realized that after David died when I was getting drunk every day like I said earlier, that was me going through a dark night of the soul and my soul was fragmented because it was trying to leave my body. The Shaman had brought my soul back down and that's why I felt great. But Philip leaving traumatized me and I went through another intense moment of the dark night of the soul which it was supposed to happen that way. Me being devastated over this all made sense now. He was triggering my abandonment issues from my childhood. I had always left the men I was with. He was the first one to leave me. It was so I had to face the trauma head on. There was no more running from healing.

I was talking to Philip on the phone when he was in New York, and I was telling him about my drug addiction being gone, and of course, he thought I was lying. I would have thought I was lying too. So, I understood.

Philip caught covid on the way to New York and he had cut his visit short and came back early. He lied to me and kept telling me he was still in New York until he sent a picture of his meds that he got from a doctor and I looked at the background and noticed he was back at home. Which then he was mad at me because he got busted lying. But at that time, I couldn't see why he lied but now that I'm back to normal I can. He had lied because I was crazy and a raging lunatic. I was sending text messages that were so mean and hurtful. I said things to him to hurt him like he had hurt me. Hurt people hurt people Just like I had learned in my previous relationships. I had turned into everything I hated without even realizing it. I said things like I was talking to Floyd and I never ever thought that way about Philip but at this point I did. No, it wasn't right to do but I was tired of being the one hurt all the time so I thought it was ok. Even though it was my actions that caused it. He thought I was a violent person which I still don't understand because I never gave him any indication that I was. But later on, I found out I was triggering one of his traumas with his mother. He couldn't stand conflict of any form because of his trauma. I didn't know this at the time.

We didn't talk for a few days. Philip at one point would try to talk about things but I wouldn't. I didn't know how to sit down and have an adult conversation about feelings. If it was done, I felt attacked or would be the one attacking.

Later on, I realized this also came from my childhood. We avoid taking responsibility; we avoid confronting in a healthy manner because we assume things won't get resolved or we will be lied to. The only time I would ever confront someone or talk was when I was blowing up and angry.

Chapter Twelve

TIME FOR CHANGE

Philip and I were not together but still talking. At one point, I had talked to a friend of mine, Jerry, in Texas. Jerry had sent me roses and I posted a picture of them on Facebook, and Philip had seen them. He was mad because I was talking to another man. I said you're living back home with your wife. I can talk to other people if I want, but I can't control it if someone sends me flowers. Well, Philip was a jealous person from what he has told me he has always been like that.

So, after that argument, I decided I was going to go up to Michigan to visit my kids for a week. When I was up there, I was helping a friend of mine move that I've known since I was 18. When I was talking to Philip, I told him who I was with, but he also later found out that this was a man that I had sex with years ago. He was really upset. I didn't tell him exactly who it was. Took me a while to be able to comprehend why he was so angry. In my eyes no big deal it's not like anything happened but I wouldn't like it either. But once again, we were still split up, so I could do as I pleased, just like he did.

I came back from Michigan early as there was a hurricane heading toward Florida, so I came back so that as soon as it passed, I could get supplies to the part of Florida that got hit. Philip was worried about me and drove to Georgia so we could wait it out there. Which was nice, and I appreciated it. We stayed in Georgia for a couple of days. When we got back, we took a Uhaul of supplies over to the Okeechobee area for hurricane victims.

Philip and I decided to get back together and move back into the house we both just moved out of. Philip had paid rent there for 6 months, we still had the keys. Things once again went downhill. I was really trying, this second time, to show emotion and talk more, but I owed Philip about $7500, and I lied and told him I had a settlement coming, and when I told him it wasn't, he was done and ready to go back home.

I understood it but was still upset. It was a lie from before him and I were even together and I never fessed up. But I was working before this. So, I planned on paying him that way, but work stopped.

The night I moved back to the cottage, I was going through another peek of the dark night of the soul. If you have never been through this, you won't understand, but if you have, then you know they can be crazy. It can actually make you feel crazy. Through my awakening, I think there were about 3 times I almost put myself in a mental hospital. But I remember laying on the couch and crying, thinking I was losing my mind. But I was talking to Philip and told him any and all lies that were told about myself, and I even told him about lies that didn't involve him. I just wanted this dark night of the soul to end. He was good about everything and said he forgave me.

He also thought I was crazy, and it was understandable because I did at times too. He made me feel ashamed of what I was going through. But a few weeks ago, I brought up that he left because he thought I was crazy, and he shrugged his shoulders. Was kind of nice to see because showed me he can't stay when things get tough. As soon as there were any problems he ran. Showed me I wasn't crazy about that thought.

I had noticed anytime I would bring up future plans or anything between us he wouldn't say a word. But he never talks about anything in the future. It's always in the past. I don't think he knew I was picking up on this but I notice everything.

After this is when I truly started working on healing myself, I was fed up with the pain in my life and hurting myself and hurting others. Jesus wasn't going to stop or back off until I did it. Today, I'm very thankful for it. I would be lying if I said I was happy at the time because I wasn't. It's hard because your whole life gets turned upside down.

During this time, I realized I was psychic and that my gifts were getting stronger. Some people believe psychics are evil and working with demons, and that is the farthest thing from the truth. We are born this way. A Demon is not going to heal me or make me better myself and tell me why he humbled me. So many people are just afraid of the unknown. I didn't ask to be this way; Jesus made me, so he made me as he wanted me.

Right before Philip and I split up, the first time, I had a dream that Philip and I were out in the desert riding on horses, and all of a sudden, a big trumpet came out of the sky and just started blaring. We weren't scared, we were both excited, and our horses were jumping around on their back legs. I woke right up, and I told Philip what had happened in my dream, and he said you had a biblical dream. I asked why would I have that? I don't have dreams like that.

He replied I don't know, but you did and then after this I started getting messages and now that I look back during my life I was getting them all along, I just didn't realize it.

Like a month before covid hit, I was talking to David and I told him that a big virus was coming and going to kill hundreds of thousands of people and he just looked at me and said oh yeah and the next month covid hit. Even though that was man-made somehow, I knew.

Another time, I asked Philip to take me to the beach, which was weird because it was just random. When we got to the beach the fire department and ambulance trucks were there. I said a young man drowned, Phillip says well God I hope not. I replied he's dead. We walked up to the police officer and Philip asked what happened they said they were looking for a young man and as we walked away I wrote R.I.P and then the letter B in the sand. Philip looked down, but he didn't say anything. Two days later he called me. He said they released the name of that boy who drowned and his name was Ben.

There are many more experiences but the point is my messages I was getting had become more frequent and stronger. I had note books of messages that I was receiving. I never took notes. I also went into reading books. I haven't read a book since I was 16. I didn't know this happens during a spiritual awakening.

Jesus strips everything away from you to make you be alone. I was very angry about this. I even had the message my work was going to stop. I had my own painting business, and I thought no way because I was really busy all the time, and sure enough, my work stopped completely.

Everyone in my life disappeared except for David's family and Philip to a certain extent. So thankful for them. They became my true family through all of this. Later I found out in my awakening that Jesus removes you from your family and puts you in isolation to learn, heal and go through ego death. Especially because our blood family will most likely talk and look down on you for the things you are saying. Heck, there are times we even feel we are crazy, so it's understandable. But he had me with people who might have thought it at times but they didn't say it.

Chapter Thirteen

TAKING MY POWER BACK

A few months ago, I had a dream. I walked up to Jesus on the cross, and he looked up at me and said I turned you into everything you hated. You had to be humbled to be humble. I woke up from that dream in tears. He did exactly that.

I've always stayed a good person in trying to help people but I did look down on drug addicts. I always said they have a weak mind, homeless people I used to say get a damn job and here I was living in David's parent's cottage jobless and I turned into my biggest pet peeve and that was a liar. My whole life was a lie, so I could feel important to someone because I didn't feel important to myself, I didn't love myself, and I couldn't see what was under the mess that I had made of myself.

I was going from relationship to relationship, trying to find someone to fill the void in me. I was sabotaging men who tried to love me because they couldn't fill the void. Some hearts I broke others I lost a part of me staying trying to make others happy and not abandon them like I was.

Well Philip and I were still hanging out but not being intimate so I figured time to start doing my own thing just as he was. Then, when I went back up to Michigan, I was going to have lunch with a male friend of mine, and I told Philip I was going to see him. Well, he sent me a text when I was up there and asked me if I was going to lunch? I said yes, I told you this. He flew off the handle and was fighting with me again. I said were not having sex, you show no emotion, you live with your wife even though they are in separate bedrooms and he swore up and down he wanted to work things out. I cancelled the lunch. I get back to Florida and NOTHING. He was right back to the same way he was before I left. This is called bread crumbing; and avoidant behavior. The person comes in all hot and heavy when they think you are moving on. Once they think they have you, it stops. He did this a few times. But when he did this, it made me have to heal all over again. Philip had traumas and baggage also to deal with. But it was also Jesus testing me to see if I valued myself and seen my self-worth yet. To see if I was picking up on what was happening and would put a stop to it. I just didn't know this at the time. I did notice what he was doing, but I just didn't say anything because I didn't want to fight and have him leave.

When I asked why we weren't having sex, he said I don't know there must be a reason. It was making me feel like I was unattractive and not good enough. And when I bring this up to this day and repeat what he said his reply is I said that? I don't remember saying that or you even asking me about it. This was his answer to many things I would bring up. He says this so he don't have to take accountability.

These are the types of games that were played all along. Anytime I would try to talk or ask questions, I would not get answers. He would give me short ones. This was done because he didn't want to fight either or take accountability. I kept trying to heal the situation because of the lies I told him. I knew I had hurt him deeply, so I kept thinking I could make this better, but now I went into a stage of over-giving and it became the more I over gave the more he pulled back. The relationship became one-sided, and I was done giving. This was God's way of saying WAKE UP, SEE YOUR SELF WORTH. LEAVE.

During all this I had realized I'm open with showing affection but I truly struggle with expressing how I feel or speaking up for myself especially with him because of the damage I already caused, I didn't want any more fights.

Well, one night, I asked him what he wanted between us, and he answered me with a question. When this happens, they are trying to avoid answering. I finally got an answer out of him, saying he thinks he needs a break. So, I gave him a break. I took my power back from the situation. I had ended it, and it was for the best for both of us.

A few months later, he thought I was moving on and came rushing back and once again I fell for it. I woke up one morning to a voice saying, you're going to keep learning your lesson until you learn it. I knew it was about Philip, but I tried to ignore it. Sure enough, within 2 months Philip was doing his pulling back again and friend zoned me again. HERE WAS MY LESSON. This is where I was learning my lesson about avoidant behavior. Any time we would start bonding he would pull back to avoid getting close. People with avoidant behavior can stay in toxic relationships for a long time because change and growth is not expected of them. That is why he was able to hold 2 long term relationships since their partner is also toxic but since I was healing my toxic traits were disappearing I expected more out of him and our relationship.

When he would come towards me he always said he had to stay married because couldn't afford a divorce because of financial reasons from when we were together. But in reality it is because he didn't want to give up his security he had with her. Avoidant people have to have someone on standby before they will leave another person. I also did this in my past. But he expected me to be in a 3rd party relationship. He never took into consideration how I felt or how it affected me. Even though Philip and his wife were not sleeping together and their marriage was broken down how could I ever feel good about myself or our relationship? But I have healed so I cannot be in that situation. I wanted our relationship to grow so he would do this to avoid it. This is where I also learned I had anxious attachment which I have now healed. I would hold on to hope of things changing because of the words he would say when he came rushing back in instead of listening to the words that were never spoke of again after a week or so and his actions weren't lining up.

I received messages during my awakening that he never wanted a relationship when this originally started. He was coming after me through lust, and that is why he got nailed with karma. I also received karma for hurting him. But with the strange things going on at my house after David died, he felt like he had to save me. But since he thought I was getting a settlement and he was going to get divorced and sell his house, he thought things would all work out.

We both learned many lessons. And have had to pay for them. I couldn't see at the time that I had used Philip to cover up the pain I was in from my past and then 2 boyfriends dying in a row. And Philip was using me to fill the void of the unhappy marriage he was in. That is the wrong reason to start any relationship.

I can say I spent almost 2 years trying to heal this relationship and the damage I had done. When the truth is I was taking blame for everything and trying to heal him when neither of us were ready for a relationship. We needed to turn inward and finish healing ourselves first. So, I realized it was time to walk away from a relationship that was not healthy for me. It doesn't mean walking away with anger like I used to. Now, I have learned everyone enters your life for a reason weather it's a lesson or a blessing, either way I now have gratitude for every one of them.

I would lose myself in relationships trying to be loved, trying to love them but in reality, I kept losing myself. When I get into relationships, I go all in instead of taking my time. I was naive with who I gave my heart to.

Jesus had sent Philip in to help me, but we were not supposed to get together at that time. We were supposed to do things the correct way. I sabotaged the hell out of that relationship by lying, But he sabotaged it by running away all the time and not healing his traumas also. So I had to stop blaming myself for everything. During our time together, it was brought to my attention that we were mirroring each other with different behaviors and patterns. What you can't stand outside of yourself look inward and see why it is triggering you. Heal and change it. Which in return it will stop showing up in your life.

I self-sabotaged in this relationship because I was expecting Philip to be like the rest of my past relationships. The truth is we could have healed and worked through our problems if we both knew how. But first you have to take accountability and look inward and not everyone is willing to do that. I sent us down a long road that should have never happened. But I always thought when he left he did it to take his power back to heal when the truth was he was running Just as I did at a certain point, I couldn't look at it like that at the time, but I can now. I didn't appreciate everything he was doing. He didn't appreciate that I kept trying to heal this/ us, and I was over giving. I constantly took the blame for everything in our relationship, and you can't do that. Relationships take two people to make it work.

It's always easy to blame everyone else for the bad things in our relationships or that he/ she left me but the truth is you need to look at what WE could have done differently.

Doesn't mean I stopped loving him, but I've done too much work on myself and healing to know I can't be in these situations anymore. I had to learn to let go.

When you or someone else runs from relationships, it's actually running from themselves/ ourselves. This was a major lesson. I always wanted to heal things because I didn't like people hurting but also because I couldn't handle the insecurities of not knowing what was going to happen. Stop chasing, love yourself, and know that whatever is meant for you will find you. But have compassion for yourself and that person. We all have a shadow side filled with traumas, pain, hurt weather inflicted by other people or yourself. It's time to quit hiding and start healing. I took my power back, and finally, once in my life, I made the best decision for myself mentally and emotionally. And did it in a healthy way.

Jesus will use people to help you, but also teach you lessons and to move you forward in life. Philip has been my biggest lesson. Sometimes, I was upset I would ask Jesus why him? At the time, it felt like it was tearing our friendship apart, and that really hurt. He was my Philip and my safe zone. The answer was because you two are best friends on the other side and very, very old souls who knew you could trigger, help, learn and teach each other lessons.

Chapter Fourteen

WHAT JESUS DID FOR ME

My story isn't a poor me story. It's a real story. I take all accountability for my actions. I'm not proud of this, but to heal I needed to see the truth. I was running from myself, running from healing emotions that I kept burying deep down and just pushing forward in life, searching and finding nothing.

Some people used to think I loved drama, but the truth is I had to fight to get any emotions out because it was the only time I felt anything. I used to have a light switch, as I call it. I could shut off my emotions whenever I felt something wasn't right, or I was going to get hurt. But after a while, I couldn't turn the switch on when I wanted to feel happy, or even love.

After David dying and I found out all that was happening and just the heartbreak of two boyfriends dying in a row, I was done. I told Jesus I never wanted anything to do with love again. I was going to be single for the rest of my life. And that is also another reason Jesus brought Philip in, was to break open my heart to heal and show me love is possible and can be a good thing. Just not in the way you expect. I was learning to love myself. You can't love other people until you love yourself first. Jesus knew I was going to fall in love with Philip. It sounds crazy to get hurt and what was done in our relationship, but it cracked my heart wide open, so I had no choice but to be alone and heal the proper way and love myself. We are not here to be rigid; we are here to follow in Jesus's footsteps and to love and be loved.

During my healing I started to wonder many times if I was a narcissist because I was told I was at times by a partner. Well, when I read up on it I thought well this sign kind of sounds like me, oh wait maybe this one to. I hated it. I felt awful. Who wants to be a narcissist? Well then I was told no, but you do have narcissist flees. I thought, what the hell is that? It's where we pick up some of the narcissistic tendencies from being in narcissistic relationships or even having narcissistic parents.

People with tenancies can change. They have to want to change and see the change that needs to be done. We can't force change on anyone. Change begins with a choice. Once they feel enough pain, it is usually when it happens. I couldn't stand myself anymore or the pain I was causing myself and the people I loved and it was time. I thought pushing forward all my life was strong, but it was actually weak of me not to take the time to heal myself so I didn't hurt others or myself.

I remember One day I got a message asking Are you strong or are you happy? I said strong, then I heard wrong answer. That hit me hard and sunk in. Jesus didn't put us here to be strong, but he put us here to find ourselves and be happy. Then you become strong, and no one or any circumstances can break you. We are here to love and be loved and to show the world unconditional love, we can't do that when we are traumatized and walking around in our shadow selves.

And this is when Jesus brought me to my knees to bring me back to life. Jesus will send angels into your life at the right time. He answers prayers in unexpected ways. He will give you lessons you didn't know you needed. He will let you experience love, sadness, anger, and hard trials to build you. He knows what your future holds.

A couple of weeks ago, I had a dream. Jason walked up and handed me a little black bag. I looked at it, and I didn't see anything, so I handed it back to him. He reached into it and handed me a gold engagement ring. He didn't ask me to marry him again. He just silently handed it to me. I put it on my finger turned and walked away, I remember looking at the ring and it being gold really stuck out to me because I don't wear gold, and the only thing I said was, what about Philip? Well, from what my message about that dream meaning was, the gold circle and spiritual meaning means new life, self-renewal, and being one with god.

I was also told I put Philip on a pedestal when I truly had to look at the fact that he wasn't perfect. Yes, I caused damage, but my response was to action, and the same was true with him. We can try to make people villains, or we are the villains, but the truth is we read energy, and if something is off, we react.

We need to see that every ending in life is a new beginning to rebuild. Most of the time we are just afraid to let go, whether that is people, pain we carry around, resentment, or the old you. It's time to forgive and release. We need to process grief; Grief doesn't actually have to be a physical death. Death of old self, death of relationships, death of any part of your life that is over with.

As you can see, I have made a complete mess of my life. The traumas I went through as a child were not my fault, but it is our job to heal them. I always thought pushing forward was the right way to go. But, of course, you don't realize what a mess you are making until it's too late.

At the beginning of my awakening, I kept hearing take your power back. For the life of me, I couldn't figure out what they were talking about since there were so many ways to take that. Now I do. They were telling me to take my power back from traumas, bad decisions, and relationships and the situation I was now in.

So, I learned that I had to look back at each trauma and feel what I needed to feel about it, sit with it for a bit, cry, scream, do what I needed to get the pain out. I had to look at whoever was involved in it, what could have made them do it, and how it affected me as a child, teenager, and adult. I had to see how it affected my decisions and relationships. And how it was still affecting me today. I HAD TO LEARN TO FORGIVE. A lot of people say no; they don't deserve forgiveness. When we forgive, it is forgiveness for ourselves, not the other person. The offender has gone on with life while we are stuck in chains. It was time to break the chains and take my power back by healing and forgiving even myself for everything I have done to myself and others. It was looking at why I went into relationships I didn't really want to be in, or why I stayed in relationships I was getting hurt in. Why was I self-sabotaging myself over and over? My trust was shot in relationships, so I didn't trust the men I had been with. I also didn't trust myself because of the choices I had made.

Don't ever be ashamed of your mistakes; They teach you how to make things right. And never regret loving someone. Love is never wasted. You are the only unconditional love people have ever known. And that person was brought into your life because they are what you needed at that time.

Your shadow self is the hell that is in your head. If you ask Jesus to help you, he will walk beside you and help heal those wounds.

I remember when this all started and Philip had left. I was on my knees just sobbing, and I said please, please take my life. I can't do this anymore. I want to die, I heard get up you have work to do, I will help you. And he kept his promise.

Some of our lessons in life can be really tough, and Jesus will keep showing you the same lesson over and over until you learn it. The scenario will be the same just different people. And this is exactly what Philip was showing me. His behavior was reflecting Floyd and David to make me heal those wounds. I didn't know that at that time. I just thought oh great here we go again.

But always, always be grateful for your lessons. As they made you stronger, wiser and now you can turn around and pass that wisdom on to help others. When we reach the top, we don't stop. We turn around and give a helping hand to someone else who is struggling.

Jesus has giving me a clean slate and giving me back my soul so I could finally be happy and at peace in my life.

It hasn't been an easy road; our healing journeys are never-ending. But I can, for once in my life, say I am proud of myself as I have pulled myself out of the darkness, and I now see the light.

With everything that has been done to me and I did to myself in my life, anytime anything good would happen in life I was always, always waiting for the other shoe to drop. My brain would automatically think negative things or someone was scheming to hurt me. So, I had to learn when I did this, I had to push the negative thought out and replace it with 2 positives. This wasn't easy to do. But your thoughts create your reality.

Now, I know in this book I have made myself out to be this bad person, but the truth is under the pain, mistakes, bad decisions, bad relationships I put myself in. The truth is I'm a good person; I'm a bold woman unafraid of challenges and taking a risk. I'm a huge animal lover and would easily go to jail to protect animals and people. I'm a hard worker; I have worked hard since I was 13 years old. Yes, I did learn that I buried myself in work to not feel pain, but I am still working on that. I'm coming out of survival mode. I am strong, Independent, and love and care for people. I help in any way I can. And when I love someone, I love them whole heartedly. We lose our identity when we don't heal, and that's a big lesson I've learned. I can love now without losing myself, as I have to love myself first. Our past does not define us. The past parts of us are illusions.

I have cried more in the last 2 years than I have in my whole life. My dad said one time when he was abusing me not to cry only babies cry, and I carried that through life. So, for the last 2 years, I've been releasing all these tears, It's the soul's way of healing. And I'm no longer holding them in. But the hardest part is over. I can now look at myself and be proud that I'm healing and the person I have become. I'm not proud of my past, but I'm healing from being ashamed of it. For it has made me who I am today. I've had to forgive myself for not healing sooner. Not loving myself and knowing I deserved better in life. For not making better decisions for myself and my kids. And to understand my actions were taught to me, I did the best I could with what I knew. But they do not define me, It's never too late to change.

We don't know people's past. And just maybe that person needs you to help them. Pray for people; Jesus works miracles every day. He has never left my side. He let me go through all of these lessons so I can now help others.

There is a reason for everything, we just need to ask what he is trying to show us and the answer will be revealed. Jesus will use people to help save you. He will give you signs everywhere to get your attention we just have to have our eyes and heart open to receive.

This hasn't been an easy book for me to write. But it's to let you know there is always hope and faith that people can change., We shouldn't judge a book by its cover.

I never understood why Jesus kept asking me to write this book, but I did as he asked. Well, today I realized it was because it's the best way to self-reflect. It's easy for us to sit here and blame everyone else for our problems in life because we don't want to see the truth. The truth is yes, as a child, I had no choice in what was happening, but as a young adult, I did. I chose not to feel the pain I was in; I chose not to get the help I needed, I chose to get into unhealthy relationships and stay in them. I chose the drugs and drinking. I chose to lie and to hurt others. I chose to continue to hurt myself. Until Jesus stepped in and said, it was time to heal.

Before my awakening, I wanted to believe Jesus existed. I mean, who doesn't want to believe in him? But now with my dreams, my drug addiction gone overnight, and the healing he put me through, I KNOW he exists.

I now know who I am as I have walked through the valley of the shadow of death. AMEN

About the Author

Jozlyn Daniels is a respected spiritual guide known for her roles as a psychic medium, healer, reiki master and shaman. With a heart full of compassion, she helps anyone she can

Driven by empathy and a belief in the power of spiritual healing, Jozlyn creates a nurturing space for her people to explore their inner selves and navigate life's challenges with resilience. Her authentic presence and intuitive guidance illuminate paths to clarity and empowerment

As an author, Jozlyn's written works provide invaluable insights for those on the spiritual journey, inviting readers to embrace their potential and connect with the magic of the universe. Through her teachings and writings, she continues to inspire countless souls on their paths of self-discovery and growth.